Published by icitybooks 2024
icitybooks.com

Cover design: icitybooks
Internal design: icityretail

ISBN 978-0-6457100-8-3

WORK DIARY

This diary belongs to:

Name
....

Address
....

....

....

Phone
....

Email
....

Recollections may vary but not with receipts

Section 1:

Diary entries

In this section, you can record any events, incidents or regular diary entries in detail. It is recommended you include all relevant information such as the location where the incident happened, the time of the event, details of anyone who may have witnessed the event and how the incident has impacted your life.

Date:	People present or witnesses:
Time: am/pm	
Location:	

Event and how it made you feel:

Date:	**People present or witnesses:**
Time: am/pm	
Location:	

Event and how it made you feel:

Date:	People present or witnesses:
Time: am/pm	
Location:	

Event and how it made you feel:

Date:	People present or witnesses:
Time: am/pm	
Location:	

Event and how it made you feel:

Date:	People present or witnesses:
Time: am/pm	
Location:	

Event and how it made you feel:

Date:	People present or witnesses:
Time: am/pm	
Location:	

Event and how it made you feel:

Date:	People present or witnesses:
Time: am/pm	
Location:	

Event and how it made you feel:

Date:	**People present or witnesses:**
Time: **am/pm**	
Location:	

Event and how it made you feel:

Date:	People present or witnesses:
Time: am/pm	
Location:	

Event and how it made you feel:

Date:	People present or witnesses:
Time: am/pm	
Location:	

Event and how it made you feel:

Date:	**People present or witnesses:**
Time: **am/pm**	
Location:	

Event and how it made you feel:

Date:	People present or witnesses:
Time: am/pm	
Location:	

Event and how it made you feel:

Date:	People present or witnesses:
Time: am/pm	
Location:	

Event and how it made you feel:

Date:	People present or witnesses:
Time: am/pm	
Location:	

Event and how it made you feel:

Date:	**People present or witnesses:**
Time: **am/pm**	
Location:	

Event and how it made you feel:

Date:	People present or witnesses:
Time: am/pm	
Location:	

Event and how it made you feel:

Date:	People present or witnesses:
Time: am/pm	
Location:	

Event and how it made you feel:

Date:	People present or witnesses:
Time: am/pm	
Location:	

Event and how it made you feel:

Date:	People present or witnesses:
Time: am/pm	
Location:	

Event and how it made you feel:

Date:	People present or witnesses:
Time: am/pm	
Location:	

Event and how it made you feel:

Date:	People present or witnesses:
Time: am/pm	
Location:	

Event and how it made you feel:

Date:	People present or witnesses:
Time: am/pm	
Location:	

Event and how it made you feel:

Date:	People present or witnesses:
Time: am/pm	
Location:	

Event and how it made you feel:

Date:	People present or witnesses:
Time: am/pm	
Location:	

Event and how it made you feel:

Date:	People present or witnesses:
Time: am/pm	
Location:	

Event and how it made you feel:

Date:	People present or witnesses:
Time: am/pm	
Location:	

Event and how it made you feel:

Date:	People present or witnesses:
Time: am/pm	
Location:	

Event and how it made you feel:

Date:	People present or witnesses:
Time: am/pm	
Location:	

Event and how it made you feel:

Date:	**People present or witnesses:**
Time: am/pm	
Location:	

Event and how it made you feel:

Date:	People present or witnesses:
Time: am/pm	
Location:	

Event and how it made you feel:

Date:	People present or witnesses:
Time: am/pm	
Location:	

Event and how it made you feel:

Date:	People present or witnesses:
Time: am/pm	
Location:	

Event and how it made you feel:

Date:	People present or witnesses:
Time: am/pm	
Location:	

Event and how it made you feel:

Date:	People present or witnesses:
Time: am/pm	
Location:	

Event and how it made you feel:

Date:	People present or witnesses:
Time: am/pm	
Location:	

Event and how it made you feel:

Date:	People present or witnesses:
Time: am/pm	
Location:	

Event and how it made you feel:

Date:	People present or witnesses:
Time: am/pm	
Location:	

Event and how it made you feel:

Date:	People present or witnesses:
Time: am/pm	
Location:	

Event and how it made you feel:

Date:	People present or witnesses:
Time: am/pm	
Location:	

Event and how it made you feel:

Date:	People present or witnesses:
Time: am/pm	
Location:	

Event and how it made you feel:

Date:	People present or witnesses:
Time: am/pm	
Location:	

Event and how it made you feel:

Date:	People present or witnesses:
Time: am/pm	
Location:	

Event and how it made you feel:

Date:	People present or witnesses:
Time: am/pm	
Location:	

Event and how it made you feel:

Date:	People present or witnesses:
Time: am/pm	
Location:	

Event and how it made you feel:

Date:	People present or witnesses:
Time: am/pm	
Location:	

Event and how it made you feel:

Date:	**People present or witnesses:**
Time: am/pm	
Location:	

Event and how it made you feel:

Date:	**People present or witnesses:**
Time: **am/pm**	
Location:	

Event and how it made you feel:

Date:	People present or witnesses:
Time: am/pm	
Location:	

Event and how it made you feel:

Date:	**People present or witnesses:**
Time: am/pm	
Location:	

Event and how it made you feel:

Date:	People present or witnesses:
Time: am/pm	
Location:	

Event and how it made you feel:

Date:	**People present or witnesses:**
Time: am/pm	
Location:	

Event and how it made you feel:

Date:	People present or witnesses:
Time: am/pm	
Location:	

Event and how it made you feel:

Date:	People present or witnesses:
Time: am/pm	
Location:	

Event and how it made you feel:

Date:	People present or witnesses:
Time: am/pm	
Location:	

Event and how it made you feel:

Date:	**People present or witnesses:**
Time: am/pm	
Location:	

Event and how it made you feel:

Date:	People present or witnesses:
Time: am/pm	
Location:	

Event and how it made you feel:

Date:	People present or witnesses:
Time: am/pm	
Location:	

Event and how it made you feel:

Date:	People present or witnesses:
Time: am/pm	
Location:	

Event and how it made you feel:

Date:	People present or witnesses:
Time: am/pm	
Location:	

Event and how it made you feel:

Date:	People present or witnesses:
Time: am/pm	
Location:	

Event and how it made you feel:

Date:	People present or witnesses:
Time: am/pm	
Location:	

Event and how it made you feel:

Date:	People present or witnesses:
Time: am/pm	
Location:	

Event and how it made you feel:

Date:	People present or witnesses:
Time: am/pm	
Location:	

Event and how it made you feel:

Date:	People present or witnesses:
Time: am/pm	
Location:	

Event and how it made you feel:

Date:	People present or witnesses:
Time: am/pm	
Location:	

Event and how it made you feel:

Date:	**People present or witnesses:**
Time: **am/pm**	
Location:	

Event and how it made you feel:

Date:	People present or witnesses:
Time: am/pm	
Location:	

Event and how it made you feel:

Date:	People present or witnesses:
Time: am/pm	
Location:	

Event and how it made you feel:

Date:	People present or witnesses:
Time: am/pm	
Location:	

Event and how it made you feel:

Date:	People present or witnesses:
Time: am/pm	
Location:	

Event and how it made you feel:

Date:	People present or witnesses:
Time: am/pm	
Location:	

Event and how it made you feel:

Date:	People present or witnesses:
Time: am/pm	
Location:	

Event and how it made you feel:

Date:	People present or witnesses:
Time: am/pm	
Location:	

Event and how it made you feel:

Date:	People present or witnesses:
Time: am/pm	
Location:	

Event and how it made you feel:

Date:	People present or witnesses:
Time: am/pm	
Location:	

Event and how it made you feel:

Date:	People present or witnesses:
Time: am/pm	
Location:	

Event and how it made you feel:

Date:	People present or witnesses:
Time: am/pm	
Location:	

Event and how it made you feel:

Date:	People present or witnesses:
Time: am/pm	
Location:	

Event and how it made you feel:

Date:	People present or witnesses:
Time: am/pm	
Location:	

Event and how it made you feel:

Date:	People present or witnesses:
Time: am/pm	
Location:	

Event and how it made you feel:

Date:	People present or witnesses:
Time: am/pm	
Location:	

Event and how it made you feel:

Date:	People present or witnesses:
Time: am/pm	
Location:	

Event and how it made you feel:

Date:	**People present or witnesses:**
Time: am/pm	
Location:	

Event and how it made you feel:

Date:	People present or witnesses:
Time: am/pm	
Location:	

Event and how it made you feel:

Date:	**People present or witnesses:**
Time: am/pm	
Location:	

Event and how it made you feel:

Date:	People present or witnesses:
Time: am/pm	
Location:	

Event and how it made you feel:

Date:	People present or witnesses:
Time: am/pm	
Location:	

Event and how it made you feel:

Date:	People present or witnesses:
Time: am/pm	
Location:	

Event and how it made you feel:

Date:	People present or witnesses:
Time: am/pm	
Location:	

Event and how it made you feel:

Date:	People present or witnesses:
Time: am/pm	
Location:	

Event and how it made you feel:

Date:	**People present or witnesses:**
Time: am/pm	
Location:	

Event and how it made you feel:

Date:	People present or witnesses:
Time: am/pm	
Location:	

Event and how it made you feel:

Date:	People present or witnesses:
Time: am/pm	
Location:	

Event and how it made you feel:

Date:	People present or witnesses:
Time: am/pm	
Location:	

Event and how it made you feel:

Date:	People present or witnesses:
Time: am/pm	
Location:	

Event and how it made you feel:

Date:	People present or witnesses:
Time: am/pm	
Location:	

Event and how it made you feel:

Date:	**People present or witnesses:**
Time: am/pm	
Location:	

Event and how it made you feel:

Date:	People present or witnesses:
Time: am/pm	
Location:	

Event and how it made you feel:

Date:	People present or witnesses:
Time: am/pm	
Location:	

Event and how it made you feel:

Date:	**People present or witnesses:**
Time: **am/pm**	
Location:	

Event and how it made you feel:

Date:	People present or witnesses:
Time: am/pm	
Location:	

Event and how it made you feel:

Date:	People present or witnesses:
Time: am/pm	
Location:	

Event and how it made you feel:

Date:	People present or witnesses:
Time: am/pm	
Location:	

Event and how it made you feel:

Date:	People present or witnesses:
Time: am/pm	
Location:	

Event and how it made you feel:

Date:	People present or witnesses:
Time: am/pm	
Location:	

Event and how it made you feel:

Date:	People present or witnesses:
Time: am/pm	
Location:	

Event and how it made you feel:

Date:	People present or witnesses:
Time: am/pm	
Location:	

Event and how it made you feel:

Date:	People present or witnesses:
Time: am/pm	
Location:	

Event and how it made you feel:

Date:	**People present or witnesses:**
Time: **am/pm**	
Location:	

Event and how it made you feel:

Date:	People present or witnesses:
Time: am/pm	
Location:	

Event and how it made you feel:

Section 2:

Lost hours due to incident worksheet

This section provides an easy way to monitor and quantify just how much time you have lost as a result of the incident(s).

You can include the date you lost the hours, the start and end time for easy verification, the number of hours lost for each particular date and the reason for the loss. The reason can be either something brief such as "off sick" or it could relate to a more detailed incident already recorded in the this diary. In the latter case, you can simply include a page number for ease of tracking.

Lost hours due to incident worksheet				
Date	**Start time**	**End time**	**Hours lost**	**Reason or page ref**

Lost hours due to incident worksheet

Date	Start time	End time	Hours lost	Reason or page ref

Lost hours due to incident worksheet				
Date	**Start time**	**End time**	**Hours lost**	**Reason or page ref**

Lost hours due to incident worksheet				
Date	Start time	End time	Hours lost	Reason or page ref

Section 3:

Doctor and specialist visits

You can record any medical visits arising from the incident(s) in this section. This includes the name of the doctor or practice, the date and time of your appointment and details of any tests you had to undertake as a result of the incident. There is room to quantify any medical costs incurred plus you can add a note reference to the page where the incident is documented.

Doctor and specialist visits

Name	Date	Time	Tests ordered	Costs	Notes ref

Doctor and specialist visits					
Name	Date	Time	Tests ordered	Costs	Notes ref

Doctor and specialist visits

Name	Date	Time	Tests ordered	Costs	Notes ref

Doctor and specialist visits					
Name	Date	Time	Tests ordered	Costs	Notes ref

Section 4:

Medications, vitamins and supplements

This section will help keep track of any medications you are taking, the frequency, quant and duration. This is an excellent way of demonstrating how the incident(s) has impacted your day to day life.

Medications, vitamins and supplements					
Name	Dosage	How often	Start date	End date	Notes

Medications, vitamins and supplements

Name	Dosage	How often	Start date	End date	Notes

Medications, vitamins and supplements

Name	Dosage	How often	Start date	End date	Notes

Medications, vitamins and supplements

Name	Dosage	How often	Start date	End date	Notes

Congratulations for taking charge of your health. Both your physical and mental health needs are important if you are to attain positive wellness and wellbeing outcomes.

You can access more resources on the following websites:

www.icitybooks.com

www.christinaosure.com (Use QR code below)

Remember:

"Recollections may vary but not with receipts!"

Made in the USA
Monee, IL
04 November 2026

67378035R00075